THE
5-MINUTE
Keto Salad
LUNCHBOX

THE 5-MINUTE *Keto Salad* LUNCHBOX

HAPPY, HEALTHY & SPEEDY
MEALS TO MAKE
IN MINUTES

ALEXANDER HART

Smith Street Books

CONTENTS

INTRODUCTION

Everybody seems to be going keto these days! The low-carb diet has taken the world by storm, and while you might assume that saying goodbye to your favourite carbs will only guarantee a bland meal come lunchtime, it doesn't have to be this way.

If you've picked up this book, chances are you already know a bit about the keto lifestyle. But if you're not yet familiar, the keto diet is a low-carb eating plan where you limit your intake of carbohydrates to between 20 and 50 grams (¾ and 1¾ oz) per day, while enjoying a higher proportion of healthy fats (from avocados, olive oil, nuts, etc.) and proteins (cheese, meat, fish, etc.), as well as plenty of healthy vegetables and keto-friendly fruits. By restricting carbohydrates to this range you put your body into a metabolic state called 'ketosis', which is where the body starts burning fat instead of glucose for energy.

Some people have found the keto diet can lead to weight loss, and it has been used to help manage some chronic health conditions. But as with all diets, it is not necessarily the best fit for everyone and it's important to talk to your local healthcare professional or doctor before embarking on a ketogenic lifestyle.

Delicious, filling and simple might not be the words that you associate with low-carb lunches, but it is possible. The speedy salads in this book will make incorporating a keto lifestyle into your daily routine completely effortless. And with 52 keto-friendly recipes to choose from, there's little chance you'll get bored. Armed with the handy tips on the following pages, it should only take you 5 or so minutes each morning to prepare a salad. You could also choose a few salads each Sunday night to meal prep and make your weekday mornings a breeze.

Keeping yourself within the 20–50 g (¾–1¾ oz) daily limit of carbohydrates generally means you'll be tracking your daily macronutrient intake. If you're leading a busy life, this can be a hurdle to going keto – but the recipes in this book have your back, with gram measurements per serving for carbs, fats and proteins given for each recipe. Keeping track of your macros has never been so easy!

SALAD INGREDIENTS

CHEESE

Many keto-friendly recipes include some sort of cheese because it's a reliable source of both protein and fat. Good-quality hard cheeses, such as parmesan and pecorino, can be purchased shaved, grated or shredded in the refrigerated section of your supermarket, which make them perfect for your 5-minute prep. Feta can be purchased ready-crumbled in tubs from most supermarkets, and fresh cheeses, such as bocconcini balls, require no preparation at all.

COOKED CHICKEN

Adding cooked chicken to your salads can be a delicious and easy way to pack a bunch of protein into your lunch. If you're short on time in the mornings, shredded cooked chicken is available from your supermarket deli. Alternatively, you could buy or cook a whole roast chicken, chop or shred the meat yourself and store it in an airtight container in the fridge for up to 4 days. Another healthy option (if you have the time) is to poach some chicken breasts for use throughout the week.

DRESSINGS

For most of the recipes in this book, the dressing is kept separately so you can dress your salad just before you eat it. You can save yourself some more time in the morning by mixing your dressing the night before and keeping the container in the fridge – you could even prep a whole week's worth in advance!

KETO-FRIENDLY FRUIT & VEG

Fruit

You won't be eating a huge amount of fruit on the keto diet due to its high carbohydrate content. However, some lower sugar fruits can be incorporated into the keto diet, these include: avocados, watermelon, strawberries, raspberries and blackberries. Fruits to avoid include: apples, bananas, grapes, mangoes and pineapple.

Vegetables

Luckily there is an abundance of vegetables that are keto-friendly, and a lot of the recipes in this book are made up of several of these vegetables, alongside a healthy serving of protein and fat. Keto-friendly vegetables include: asparagus, broccoli, cabbage,

capsicum (bell pepper), cauliflower, celery, cucumber and zucchini (courgette). Vegetables to avoid include: beetroot (beet), sweet corn, parsnip, potato and sweet potato.

HARD-BOILED EGGS

Eggs are packed full of nutrients, which make them a great protein source for keto-friendly meals. Make a batch of hard-boiled eggs ahead of time and keep them in the fridge for up to 1 week. To prepare, place your eggs in a saucepan and cover with cold water. Bring to the boil over medium–high heat, then cover, remove from the heat and set aside for 8–11 minutes (depending on how hard-boiled you like them – 8 minutes will yield a jammier yolk, while 11 minutes will give you a true hard-boiled egg). Drain, cool in iced water and peel just before adding to your salad.

NOODLES & RICE

Shirataki noodles

Made from an Asian root vegetable known as konjac, shirataki noodles are very low in carbohydrates and calories, making them a great replacement for regular noodles for those following

a keto diet. Somewhat translucent, they resemble rice vermicelli and are widely available in supermarkets. They are vegan, gluten free and contain water-soluble dietary fibre.

Veggie 'noodles'

At one stage, the only low-carb replacement for pasta were zucchini (courgette) 'zoodles' – but now there are many other options for creating vegetable-based 'noodles'. Arm yourself with a good-quality spiraliser and almost any hard, keto-friendly vegetable can be spiralised into healthy noodles! You could also use a vegetable peeler or a mandoline to make thicker ribbon noodles for something different.

Veggie 'rice'

Cauliflower rice is a popular low-carb replacement for regular rice, but vegetables, such as broccoli, can also be transformed into low-carb rice by pulsing in a food processor to a coarse, crumbly texture. Alternatively, use a large knife or a box grater to achieve similar results. Enjoy veggie rice raw or blanch it in boiling water for 30 seconds or until just cooked through, then strain and chill in an ice bath to stop the cooking process.

MINCED GARLIC & GINGER

Available in jars – or tubes (usually sold as 'paste') – from the supermarket, pre-prepared minced garlic and ginger really are a time-saving wonder. Alternatively, you can make your own: blitz a large quantity of fresh garlic or ginger in a food processor with a little water, salt and a drop of oil. It will keep well in an airtight container in the fridge for up to 2 weeks, or pressed flat in a zip-lock bag and stored in the freezer for up to 2 months.

PRE-CUT VEGETABLES

Supermarkets now carry a large range of packaged pre-cut vegetables that keep really well in your fridge, which can help keep your prep time down. Look for broccoli or cauliflower 'rice'; shredded carrot, cabbage and lettuce; spiralised zucchini/courgettes (zoodles/courgetti); and other convenient combination products, such as coleslaw and mixed salad leaves.

TOASTED NUTS & SEEDS

Toast nuts and seeds ahead of time, then leave to cool completely and store in an airtight container in your pantry for up to 1 month.

NOTES ON THE RECIPES

While the recipes in this book are designed to be simple and quick to prepare, do ensure you read through the entire recipe before starting.

NOTES ON QUANTITIES

Because it is important to limit your daily carbohydrate intake on the keto diet, you might find it helpful to weigh out your ingredients with a scale as you prepare your lunches. The recipes in this book mostly supply ingredient quantities by weight to make this easy; however, we have occasionally called for a 'handful' of something to keep your lunch prep quick and easy.

Note that the macronutrient breakdown of each salad is based on the recipe as written, but feel free to adjust the quantities to make use of what you might already have in your fridge.

All tablespoons are 15 ml (3 teaspoons/½ fl oz).

VEGE-
TABLES

GRILLED HALOUMI & BROCCOLINI SALAD

~~~

Haloumi is a salty cheese that has a high melting point, which makes it perfect for grilling or frying. It's also full of protein and a good source of fat, making it a great way to bulk out a keto lunch. Feel free to replace it with feta or ricotta salata for a quicker no-cook option.

◇◇◇◇◇◇◇◇◇◇◇

Net carbs: 12 g | Protein: 29 g | Fat: 61 g

100 g (3½ oz) haloumi, sliced

1 tablespoon olive oil

100 g (3½ oz) broccolini florets, blanched and cooled

30 g (¾ cup) rocket (arugula) leaves

2 tablespoons pomegranate seeds

1 tablespoon dukkah

CREAMY LEMON & SHALLOT VINAIGRETTE

1 tablespoon lemon juice

1 tablespoon extra virgin olive oil

1 tablespoon dijonnaise

2 teaspoons chopped shallot

salt and pepper, to taste

1. Fry the haloumi in the olive oil for 1–2 minutes on each side, until golden.

2. Toss the remaining salad ingredients together, tip into your lunchbox and top with the haloumi.

3. Combine the dressing ingredients in a small jar or container with a tight-fitting lid.

4. Pour the dressing over the salad just before serving and toss well.

MEDITERRANEAN SALAD

~~~~~~

This salad is a great way to use up all of your favourite ingredients from your local Mediterranean delicatessen. Feel free to play around and add your other favourites – marinated artichoke hearts would be great here, and some pepperoncini would add some nice heat, too.

◇◇◇◇◇◇◇◇◇◇

Net carbs: 17 g | Protein: 15 g | Fat: 29 g

100 g (⅔ cup) chopped red capsicum (bell pepper)

90 g (½ cup) chopped cucumber

50 g (1¾ oz) bocconcini

20 g (¾ oz) sun-dried tomatoes in olive oil

8 olives, pitted

30 g (¾ cup) rocket (arugula) leaves

GARLIC VINAIGRETTE

1 tablespoon extra virgin olive oil

2 teaspoons red wine vinegar

1 teaspoon dijon mustard

¼ teaspoon minced garlic

salt and pepper, to taste

1 Toss the salad ingredients together and tip into your lunchbox.

2 Whisk the dressing ingredients until smooth, then place in a small jar or container with a tight-fitting lid.

3 Pour the dressing over the salad just before serving and toss well.

KALE SALAD

Blue cheese lovers, this dressing is for you! Here it pairs perfectly with the kale and avocado for a flavoursome and nutrient-packed lunch. This salad is also great with a handful of baby spinach added.

✧✧✧✧✧✧✧✧✧✧✧

Net carbs: 8 g | Protein: 11 g | Fat: 37 g

½ avocado, diced

70 g (1 cup) finely chopped kale

6 cherry tomatoes, halved

1 tablespoon chopped toasted hazelnuts

1 tablespoon mixed seeds, such as sunflower and pepitas (pumpkin seeds)

BLUE CHEESE DRESSING

2 tablespoons crumbled blue cheese

1 tablespoon sour cream

1 tablespoon mayonnaise

2 teaspoons lemon juice

salt and pepper, to taste

1 Toss the salad ingredients together and tip into your lunchbox.

2 Whisk the dressing ingredients until smooth, then place in a small jar or container with a tight-fitting lid.

3 Pour the dressing over the salad just before serving and toss well.

BROCCOLI SALAD

≈≈≈

Here's a great salad for using up left-over cooked broccoli from last night's dinner. The dressing calls for dijonnaise – a blend of dijon mustard and mayonnaise – which you can find in delicatessens and supermarkets.

◇◇◇◇◇◇◇◇◇◇◇

Net carbs: 12 g | Protein: 19 g | Fat: 34 g

150 g (5½ oz) broccoli, cut into bite-sized florets, blanched and cooled

50 g (½ cup) grated cheddar

handful of baby spinach leaves

½ tablespoon toasted slivered almonds

½ tablespoon toasted sunflower seeds

CREAMY MUSTARD DRESSING

2 tablespoons dijonnaise

1 tablespoon Greek-style yoghurt

2 teaspoons apple cider vinegar

1 teaspoon chopped chives

salt and pepper, to taste

1 Toss the salad ingredients together and tip into your lunchbox.

2 Combine the dressing ingredients in a small jar or container with a tight-fitting lid.

3 Pour the dressing over the salad just before serving and toss well.

GOAT'S CHEESE SALAD WITH MIXED GREENS

~

This is a riff on a classic French goat's cheese salad, with crunchy toasted walnuts and sweet but tart raspberries. You can easily swap the mixed salad greens for baby spinach leaves if you prefer.

◇◇◇◇◇◇◇◇◇◇

Net carbs: 4 g | Protein: 13 g | Fat: 40 g

60 g (2 oz) goat's cheese, sliced

55 g (1½ cups) mixed salad greens

30 g (¼ cup) raspberries

2 tablespoons chopped toasted walnuts

BALSAMIC VINAIGRETTE

2 tablespoons extra virgin olive oil

1 tablespoon finely chopped red onion

1 teaspoon balsamic vinegar

1 teaspoon red wine vinegar

salt and pepper, to taste

1. Toss the salad ingredients together and tip into your lunchbox.

2. Combine the dressing ingredients in a small jar or container with a tight-fitting lid.

3. Pour the dressing over the salad just before serving and toss well.

CREAMY CAULIFLOWER 'POTATO' SALAD

~~~~~~

Potatoes are a keto no-no because of their high carb content, so here they're substituted for cooked cauliflower florets to keep things keto-friendly. You can also add some cooked bacon to further bump up the protein.

◇◇◇◇◇◇◇◇◇◇

Net carbs: 6 g | **Protein:** 11 g | **Fat:** 16 g

150 g (5½ oz) cauliflower, cut into small florets, blanched and cooled

1 hard-boiled egg, chopped

1 celery stalk, diced

1 tablespoon diced dill pickle

1 tablespoon diced red onion

20 g (½ cup) rocket (arugula) leaves

CREAMY AVO DRESSING

¼ avocado, diced

2 tablespoons sour cream or mayonnaise

1 tablespoon chopped dill

2 teaspoons apple cider vinegar

salt and pepper, to taste

1 Combine the cauliflower in a bowl with the egg, celery, dill pickle and onion.

2 Blitz the dressing ingredients together in a small blender and toss through the cauliflower mixture.

3 Place the rocket in your lunchbox and top with the creamy cauliflower salad.

VEGGIE CHOPPED SALAD

A simple chopped salad is a great way to pack so much nutritional goodness into your midday meal. If you're not a blue cheese lover you can easily replace it with feta or goat's cheese, or even avocado if you want to make this salad dairy-free.

◇◇◇◇◇◇◇◇◇◇

Net carbs: 5 g | **Protein:** 20 g | **Fat:** 51 g

1 hard-boiled egg, quartered

1 celery stalk, chopped

3 radishes, chopped

50 g (1½ cups) chopped cos (romaine) lettuce

50 g (1¾ oz) blue cheese, crumbled

1 tablespoon chopped toasted almonds

SHALLOT & MUSTARD VINAIGRETTE

2 tablespoons extra virgin olive oil

1 tablespoon red wine vinegar

2 teaspoons minced shallot

½ teaspoon dijon mustard

salt and pepper, to taste

1. Toss the salad ingredients together and tip into your lunchbox.

2. Combine the dressing ingredients in a small jar or container with a tight-fitting lid.

3. Pour the dressing over the salad just before serving and toss well.

WATERCRESS, STRAWBERRY & CUCUMBER SALAD

This is a simple and refreshing salad that is perfect for the summer months. Keto-friendly strawberries add a sweet brightness which pair perfectly with the richness of the toasted macadamia nuts.

◇◇◇◇◇◇◇◇◇◇

Net carbs: 12 g | **Protein:** 6 g | **Fat:** 12 g

½ short cucumber, sliced

75 g (½ cup) strawberries, hulled and sliced

50 g (1½ cups) watercress leaves

small handful of mint leaves

2 tablespoons chopped toasted macadamia nuts

LEMON YOGHURT DRESSING

3 tablespoons Greek-style yoghurt

2 teaspoons lemon juice

pinch of lemon zest

1 Toss the salad ingredients together and tip into your lunchbox.

2 Combine the dressing ingredients in a small jar or container with a tight-fitting lid.

3 Pour the dressing over the salad just before serving and toss well.

BERRY ENDIVE SALAD

~~~~~

Fruit is generally quite high in carbs, so it doesn't often feature in a keto diet – but berries are an exception to the rule. This salad makes glorious use of them, pairing sweet raspberries, strawberries and blackberries with creamy goat's cheese and crunchy endive.

◇◇◇◇◇◇◇◇◇◇

Net carbs: 9 g | Protein: 16 g | Fat: 37 g

125 g (4½ oz) mixed berries (raspberry, strawberry & blackberry)

60 g (2 oz) red endive leaves

60 g (2 oz) herbed goat's cheese, crumbled

2 tablespoons chopped toasted walnuts

BALSAMIC MUSTARD VINAIGRETTE

1 tablespoon extra virgin olive oil

1 teaspoon red wine vinegar

1 teaspoon balsamic vinegar

1 teaspoon dijon mustard

salt and pepper, to taste

1. Toss the salad ingredients together and tip into your lunchbox.

2. Combine the dressing ingredients in a small jar or container with a tight-fitting lid.

3. Pour the dressing over the salad just before serving and toss well.

NOODLES
+ RICE

SMOKED TOFU 'SPRING ROLL' SALAD

This is a low-carb spin on a classic Vietnamese rice noodle salad, also called bún. Here we have used smoked tofu to add extra flavour with no extra effort. You'll find it in the vegetarian section of the supermarket.

Net carbs: 17 g | Protein: 27 g | Fat: 26 g

85 g (3 oz) smoked tofu, drained and diced

70 g (½ cup) shirataki noodles, prepared as per packet instructions

1 short cucumber, spiralised

¼ red capsicum (bell pepper), sliced

40 g (¼ cup) grated carrot

1 spring onion (scallion), sliced

small handful of mint leaves

small handful of coriander (cilantro) leaves

ALMOND BUTTER DRESSING

2 tablespoons almond butter

2 teaspoons tamari sauce or coconut aminos

2 teaspoons lime juice

½ teaspoon minced ginger

1. Toss the salad ingredients together and tip into your lunchbox.

2. Whisk the dressing ingredients until smooth, then place in a small jar or container with a tight-fitting lid.

3. Pour the dressing over the salad just before serving and toss well.

CUCUMBER NOODLES WITH CREAMY DILL DRESSING

Sugar snap peas are a great way to add a little sweetness to your lunchtime – without also adding heaps of carbs. The creamy, tangy dill dressing pairs with the pepperiness of the radish and rocket perfectly.

◇◇◇◇◇◇◇◇◇◇◇

Net carbs: 12 g | Protein: 4 g | Fat: 5 g

1 short cucumber, spiralised

50 g (1¾ oz) sugar snap peas

2 radishes, sliced

30 g (¾ cup) rocket (arugula) leaves

small handful of mint leaves

CREAMY DILL DRESSING

2 tablespoons sour cream

1 tablespoon chopped dill

1 tablespoon finely diced red onion

1 tablespoon lemon juice

salt and pepper, to taste

1. Toss the salad ingredients together and tip into your lunchbox.

2. Combine the dressing ingredients in a small jar or container with a tight-fitting lid.

3. Pour the dressing over the salad just before serving and toss well.

ZUCCHINI SALAD WITH PARMESAN & MUSHROOMS

Mushrooms and parmesan are a classic pairing…
and are perfect on top of zoodles for a speedy
and tasty low-carb 'pasta' lunch!

◇◇◇◇◇◇◇◇◇◇◇

Net carbs: 10 g | Protein: 22 g | Fat: 46 g

1 tablespoon salted butter

40 g (1½ oz) button mushrooms,
sliced

pinch of dried chilli flakes

sea salt and cracked black pepper,
to taste

1 zucchini (courgette), spiralised

40 g (⅓ cup) shaved parmesan

small handful of parsley leaves

1 tablespoon toasted pine nuts

1 tablespoon toasted chopped
almonds

LEMON MUSTARD VINAIGRETTE

1 tablespoon extra virgin olive oil

1 tablespoon lemon juice

1 teaspoon dijon mustard

¼ teaspoon minced garlic

salt and pepper, to taste

1 Melt the butter in a frying pan and sauté the mushrooms over high heat for about 3 minutes, until golden. Season with chilli flakes, salt and pepper.

2 Toss the remaining salad ingredients together, tip into your lunchbox and top with the mushrooms.

3 Combine the dressing ingredients in a small jar or container with a tight-fitting lid.

4 Pour the dressing over the salad just before serving and toss well.

ITALIAN CAULIFLOWER 'RICE' SALAD

Cauliflower rice is a staple for keto dieters. It is available ready-made from some supermarkets and green grocers, or you can easily prepare it yourself. Either grate fresh cauliflower with a box grater or pulse it in a food processor.

Net carbs: 10 g | Protein: 20 g | Fat: 40 g

150 g (1½ cups) cauliflower rice

6 cherry tomatoes, halved or quartered

6 marinated pitted olives, sliced

30 g (¼ cup) shaved parmesan

1½ tablespoons toasted pine nuts

small handful of basil leaves

salt and pepper, to taste

lemon wedge, to serve

LEMON PESTO DRESSING

3 tablespoons store-bought basil pesto

1 tablespoon lemon juice

1. Toss the salad ingredients together, except the lemon wedge, and tip into your lunchbox. Add the lemon wedge.

2. Combine the dressing ingredients in a small jar or container with a tight-fitting lid.

3. Squeeze the lemon wedge over the salad just before serving. Pour the dressing over and toss well to combine.

GREEK CUCUMBER NOODLES

This fresh salad has all the classic flavours of a traditional Greek salad, but with an extra hit of protein from the tzatziki in the dressing.

Net carbs: 15 g | Protein: 11 g | Fat: 17 g

1 large cucumber, spiralised

6 cherry tomatoes, halved or quartered

50 g (1¾ oz) feta, diced

10 kalamata olives

35 g (1 cup) chopped cos (romaine) lettuce

small handful of parsley leaves

LEMONY TZATZIKI DRESSING

2 tablespoons store-bought tzatziki dip

1 tablespoon lemon juice

pepper, to taste

1. Toss the salad ingredients together and tip into your lunchbox.

2. Combine the dressing ingredients in a small jar or container with a tight-fitting lid, thinning it with a little water if desired.

3. Pour the dressing over the salad just before serving and toss well.

ANTIPASTO PASTA SALAD

Konjac pasta – also known as shirataki noodles – is now available from many supermarkets and is a great low-carb alternative to traditional pasta.

Net carbs: 8 g | Protein: 3 g | Fat: 25 g

125 g (4½ oz) konjac pasta, prepared as per packet instructions

60 g (2 oz) roasted red capsicum (bell pepper), sliced

8 marinated olives

2 marinated artichoke hearts, quartered

handful of mixed basil and parsley leaves

1 tablespoon diced pepperoncini (marinated hot yellow peppers)

ITALIAN VINAIGRETTE

1 tablespoon extra virgin olive oil

1 tablespoon red wine vinegar

½ teaspoon dijon mustard

¼ teaspoon minced garlic

¼ teaspoon dried Italian herbs

1. Toss the salad ingredients together and tip into your lunchbox.

2. Combine the dressing ingredients in a small jar or container with a tight-fitting lid.

3. Pour the dressing over the salad just before serving and toss well.

MEXICAN BROCCOLI 'RICE' SALAD

This is a low-carb version of a burrito bowl, but with high-fibre broccoli rice as the base. The dressing is almost like a guacamole ... but nobody would blame you if you felt inclined to add a few more slices of avocado on top!

Net carbs: 13 g | Protein: 16 g | Fat: 23 g

150 g (1½ cups) broccoli rice

50 g (⅓ cup) chopped red capsicum (bell pepper)

40 g (1½ oz) shredded Monterey Jack cheese

small handful of coriander (cilantro) leaves

1 tablespoon chopped pickled jalapeño

1 tablespoon finely diced red onion

dried chilli flakes, to taste

AVOCADO LIME DRESSING

¼ avocado

2 tablespoons lime juice

2 tablespoons sour cream

½ teaspoon chipotle chilli powder or taco seasoning

splash of pickled jalapeño liquid

salt and pepper, to taste

1 Toss the salad ingredients together and tip into your lunchbox.

2 Combine the dressing ingredients in a small blender and blitz until smooth and creamy. Pour into a container with a tight-fitting lid.

3 Pour the dressing over the salad just before serving and toss well.

SMOKED CHICKEN WITH HERBS & ZOODLES

Smoky, zingy, salty and fresh – this is a flavour-packed salad that's sure to have you looking forward to lunchtime! Zoodles are a great way to bulk up your meal while keeping your net carbs down.

Net carbs: 12 g | Protein: 38 g | Fat: 43 g

1 zucchini (courgette), spiralised

120 g (4½ oz) smoked chicken breast, sliced

6 cherry tomatoes, halved

50 g (⅓ cup) crumbled feta

8 marinated green olives

small handful of parsley leaves

small handful of basil leaves

LEMON VINAIGRETTE

1½ tablespoons extra virgin olive oil

1 tablespoon lemon juice

salt and pepper, to taste

1. Toss the salad ingredients together and tip into your lunchbox.

2. Combine the dressing ingredients in a small jar or container with a tight-fitting lid.

3. Pour the dressing over the salad just before serving and toss well.

TUNA NOODLES WITH SOY GINGER DRESSING

You may have said goodbye to rice noodles on the keto diet, but it doesn't mean noodle salads are entirely out of the question. Cooling cucumber ribbons and slippery shirataki noodles cut through this chilli-packed dish for a perfectly balanced, refreshing summer salad.

◇◇◇◇◇◇◇◇◇◇◇

Net carbs: 11 g | Protein: 20 g | Fat: 22 g

1 short cucumber, spiralised

95 g (3¼ oz) tinned chilli tuna in oil, drained

handful of thinly sliced red cabbage

70 g (½ cup) shirataki noodles, prepared as per packet instructions

2 teaspoons toasted sesame seeds

1 teaspoon red chilli, sliced

GINGER CHILLI DRESSING

1 tablespoon sesame oil

2 teaspoons rice wine vinegar

1 teaspoon tamari or soy sauce

½ teaspoon minced ginger

1 small red chilli, sliced

1. Toss the salad ingredients together and tip into your lunchbox.

2. Combine the dressing ingredients in a small jar or container with a tight-fitting lid.

3. Pour the dressing over the salad just before serving and toss well.

THAI-STYLE BEEF NOODLE SALAD

Using roast beef from your supermarket deli is the secret to making this Thai-style beef salad a 5-minute lunchbox wonder. A common carb replacement for keto dieters, shirataki noodles have almost no taste, soaking up the punchy flavours of the lime chilli dressing perfectly.

◇◇◇◇◇◇◇◇◇◇

Net carbs: 10 g | **Protein:** 24 g | **Fat:** 23 g

---

125 g (4½ oz) shirataki noodles, prepared as per packet instructions

100 g (3½ oz) sliced roast beef

handful of thinly sliced red cabbage

¼ red capsicum (bell pepper), sliced

small handful of Vietnamese mint leaves

small handful of coriander (cilantro) leaves

1 tablespoon chopped roasted peanuts

LIME CHILLI DRESSING

1 tablespoon toasted sesame oil

2 teaspoons lime juice

pinch of lime zest

1 teaspoon fish sauce

1 teaspoon soy sauce

½ teaspoon chilli sambal or fresh chopped chilli

1 Toss the salad ingredients together and tip into your lunchbox.

2 Combine the dressing ingredients in a small jar or container with a tight-fitting lid.

3 Pour the dressing over the salad just before serving and toss well.

CHICKEN

GREEN GODDESS CHICKEN & AVO SALAD

This salad is a combination of two classics: green goddess dressing and chicken salad. Blitzing together avocado and mayonnaise makes for the easiest green goddess dressing that's high in healthy fats. Making a batch of the dressing the night before will make prep in the morning that much easier.

◇◇◇◇◇◇◇◇◇◇

Net carbs: 4 g | Protein: 33 g | Fat: 29 g

100 g (3½ oz) shredded cooked chicken

1 celery stalk, diced

1 spring onion (scallion), sliced

small handful of mixed herbs, such as dill, tarragon, chives and parsley

55 g (1½ cups) mixed salad greens

GREEN GODDESS DRESSING

¼ avocado, diced

2 tablespoons mayonnaise

2 teaspoons lemon juice

salt and pepper, to taste

1. Combine the dressing ingredients in a small blender and blitz until smooth and creamy.

2. Combine the chicken, celery, spring onion and herbs in a bowl. Pour the dressing over and toss together.

3. Place the salad leaves in your lunchbox and top with the chicken mixture.

SESAME CABBAGE CHICKEN SLAW

This light, fresh salad is perfect year round, but is especially suited to the summer months. Brazil nuts are among the lowest-carb nuts, making them a great option for keto dieters. Now that's something to go nuts about!

◇◇◇◇◇◇◇◇◇◇

Net carbs: 10 g | **Protein:** 45 g | **Fat:** 42 g

120 g (4½ oz) shredded cooked chicken

handful of thinly shredded red cabbage

small handful of coriander (cilantro) leaves

2 tablespoons chopped Brazil nuts

2 teaspoons toasted sesame seeds

SESAME MISO DRESSING

1½ tablespoons toasted sesame oil

1 tablespoon rice wine vinegar

1½ teaspoons white (shiro) miso paste

1 teaspoon tamari sauce

1 teaspoon water

½ teaspoon minced ginger

1. Toss the salad ingredients together and tip into your lunchbox.

2. Combine the dressing ingredients in a small jar or container with a tight-fitting lid.

3. Pour the dressing over the salad just before serving and toss well.

SPICY ROAST CHICKEN CABBAGE SALAD

Crunchy, smoky, moreish, this salad is the perfect use for left-over roast chicken. The dressing has some robust flavours, but is surprisingly balanced – with sweetness from the coconut yoghurt, fattiness from the almond butter, tanginess from the lime and a bit of heat from the sriracha.

Net carbs: 16 g | Protein: 38 g | Fat: 35 g

120 g (4½ oz) shredded roast chicken

100 g (⅔ cup) sliced red and yellow capsicum (bell pepper)

handful of thinly shredded cabbage

2 tablespoons toasted sliced almonds

1 small red chilli, sliced

SPICY COCONUT DRESSING

2 tablespoons coconut yoghurt

1 tablespoon almond butter

1 tablespoon lime juice

1 teaspoon sriracha chilli sauce

1. Toss the salad ingredients together and tip into your lunchbox.

2. Whisk the dressing ingredients until smooth, then place in a small jar or container with a tight-fitting lid.

3. Pour the dressing over the salad just before serving and toss well.

CURRIED CHICKEN SALAD

A generous pinch of curry powder transforms this chicken salad into a flavour-packed lunchtime staple. Using Greek yoghurt instead of mayonnaise to bind the salad is a great way to increase your protein and ensure you're getting plenty of healthy fats.

◇◇◇◇◇◇◇◇◇◇

Net carbs: 3 g | **Protein:** 41 g | **Fat:** 11 g

2 tablespoons Greek-style yoghurt

1 teaspoon apple cider vinegar

½ teaspoon curry powder

120 g (4½ oz) shredded cooked chicken

salt and pepper, to taste

1 celery stalk, sliced

large handful of sliced radicchio leaves

1 tablespoon chopped pecans

1 tablespoon finely diced red onion

1. In a bowl, whisk together the yoghurt, vinegar and curry powder.

2. Add the chicken, toss to coat and season with salt and pepper.

3. Add the remaining ingredients to your lunchbox and top with the curried chicken.

SMOKED CHICKEN, PECAN & WATERCRESS SALAD

Smoked chicken is a beautifully simple way to bring a smoky flavour to a salad without a ton of fuss. You can buy it from butchers, delis and supermarkets. Here it pairs beautifully with peppery watercress and tangy goat's cheese.

Net carbs: 5 g | Protein: 37 g | Fat: 53 g

120 g (4½ oz) smoked chicken breast, sliced

50 g (⅓ cup) shaved fennel

40 g (1½ oz) goat's cheese, crumbled

handful of watercress leaves

2 tablespoons roughly chopped pecans

WHOLEGRAIN MUSTARD VINAIGRETTE

2 tablespoons extra virgin olive oil

1 tablespoon lemon juice

1 teaspoon wholegrain mustard

salt and pepper, to taste

1. Toss the salad ingredients together and tip into your lunchbox.

2. Combine the dressing ingredients in a small jar or container with a tight-fitting lid.

3. Pour the dressing over the salad just before serving and toss well.

CHICKEN, ASPARAGUS & BRIE SALAD

This salad is perfect in spring when asparagus is at its peak. Creamy brie adds plenty of flavour, along with some protein and fats.

Net carbs: 4 g | Protein: 47 g | Fat: 46 g

100 g (3½ oz) cooked chicken breast, sliced

50 g (1¾ oz) raw asparagus spears, woody ends trimmed, thinly sliced

50 g (1¾ oz) brie, sliced

30 g (¾ cup) rocket (arugula) leaves

2 tablespoons toasted flaked almonds

LEMON CHIVE VINAIGRETTE

1½ tablespoons extra virgin olive oil

2 teaspoons chopped chives

2 teaspoons lemon juice

pinch of lemon zest

1 teaspoon dijon mustard

salt and pepper, to taste

1. Toss the salad ingredients together and tip into your lunchbox.

2. Combine the dressing ingredients in a small jar or container with a tight-fitting lid.

3. Pour the dressing over the salad just before serving and toss well.

CHICKEN SAUSAGE, BROCCOLI & CAPSICUM SALAD

Here's a brilliant way to use up any left-over chicken sausages from last night's dinner. Jarred roasted red capsicums are used here for ease, but any left-over roasted low-carb vegetables would work instead.

◇◇◇◇◇◇◇◇◇◇

Net carbs: 9 g | **Protein:** 18 g | **Fat:** 45 g

100 g (3½ oz) left-over cooked chicken sausages, sliced

50 g (1¾ oz) broccoli florets, blanched and cooled

1 roasted red capsicum (bell pepper) marinated in olive oil, drained and sliced

75 g (1½ cups) baby spinach leaves

8 marinated olives, pitted

ITALIAN VINAIGRETTE

2 tablespoons extra virgin olive oil

1 tablespoon red wine vinegar

½ teaspoon dried Italian herbs

salt and pepper, to taste

1. Toss the salad ingredients together and tip into your lunchbox.

2. Combine the dressing ingredients in a small jar or container with a tight-fitting lid.

3. Pour the dressing over the salad just before serving and toss well.

SPICED CHICKEN LETTUCE CUPS

~~~

Here the iconic Cantonese dish san choy bau is given a slightly South-East Asian twist. Flakes of coconut, which have been toasted in a dry frying pan until fragrant and golden brown, add a low-carb, high-fat crunchy element. Dress the lettuce cups with the chicken salad just before you're ready to eat.

◇◇◇◇◇◇◇◇◇

Net carbs: 13 g | Protein: 46 g | Fat: 21 g

120 g (4½ oz) shredded cooked chicken

90 g (½ cup) diced short cucumber

handful of mixed Asian herbs, such as Thai basil, Vietnamese mint and coriander (cilantro)

5 baby cos (romaine) lettuce leaves

2 tablespoons toasted flaked coconut

lime wedge, to serve

CREAMY LIME CHILLI DRESSING

2 tablespoons coconut yoghurt

1 tablespoon lime juice

1 tablespoon almond butter

1 teaspoon sriracha or hot sauce

1. In a bowl, whisk together all the dressing ingredients.

2. Add the chicken, cucumber and herbs to the dressing and toss to combine.

3. Pop the salad into your lunchbox and store the lettuce leaves and toasted flaked coconut separately.

4. Spoon the chicken mixture into your lettuce leaves just before serving and sprinkle with the toasted coconut and a squeeze of lime juice.

CHICKEN RANCH SALAD

~~~~~

The classic American ranch dressing is naturally quite high in fats and proteins, making it perfectly suited for the keto diet. It's a staple dressing that could be used with many of the recipes in this book.

◇◇◇◇◇◇◇◇◇◇

Net carbs: 7 g | Protein: 33 g | Fat: 25 g

100 g (3½ oz) shredded cooked chicken

3 radishes, sliced

5 heirloom cherry tomatoes, halved

50 g (1½ cups) chopped cos (romaine) lettuce

40 g (¼ cup) grated carrot

RANCH DRESSING

2 tablespoons mayonnaise

1 tablespoon buttermilk

1 tablespoon mixed chopped herbs, such as dill, chives and parsley

salt and pepper, to taste

1 Toss the salad ingredients together and tip into your lunchbox.

2 Combine the dressing ingredients in a small jar or container with a tight-fitting lid.

3 Pour the dressing over the salad just before serving and toss well.

CHICKEN CAPRESE

The Italian caprese salad is a universal favourite for a reason, and adding some left-over roasted or poached chicken is an easy way to pump up the protein even further. Burrata is an Italian fresh cheese made from mozzarella that is filled with cream. You'll find it in most supermarkets, or it can be substituted with bocconcini.

Net carbs: 8 g | **Protein:** 48 g | **Fat:** 37 g

2 tomatoes, sliced

120 g (4½ oz) cooked chicken breast, sliced

50 g (1¾ oz) burrata, torn

handful of mixed salad greens

small handful of basil leaves

BALSAMIC SHALLOT VINAIGRETTE

1½ tablespoons extra virgin olive oil

2 teaspoons red wine vinegar

1 teaspoon balsamic vinegar

1 teaspoon finely chopped shallot

salt and pepper, to taste

1. Toss the salad ingredients together and tip into your lunchbox.

2. Combine the dressing ingredients in a small jar or container with a tight-fitting lid.

3. Pour the dressing over the salad just before serving and toss well.

FISH + SEAFOOD

CREAMY, CRUNCHY TUNA SALAD

Tuna salad is a lunchtime favourite for a reason, and here's a delicious keto-friendly version. Chopped toasted macadamias add a crunchy element, and as a bonus, the nuts are naturally high in healthy monounsaturated fats, which have been linked with lowering levels of LDL ('bad') cholesterol.

Net carbs: 5 g | **Protein:** 24 g | **Fat:** 33 g

125 g (4½ oz) tinned tuna slices in olive oil, drained

1 celery stalk, diced

60 g (⅓ cup) diced short cucumber

2 tablespoons mayonnaise

1½ teaspoons chopped dill pickle

1½ teaspoons chopped chives

1½ teaspoons chopped dill

2 teaspoons lemon juice

salt and pepper, to taste

4 cos (romaine) lettuce leaves

1 tablespoon chopped toasted macadamia nuts

1 In a bowl, mix together all the ingredients except the lettuce leaves and macadamias.

2 Spoon the tuna mixture into the lettuce leaves, sprinkle with the toasted macadamia nuts and pop into your lunchbox.

'CAJUN' SALMON SALAD

Influenced by French and Southern US cooking styles, Cajun cuisine is a culinary staple of the state of Louisiana. Cajun seasoning generally contains paprika, garlic powder, onion powder, cayenne pepper and salt. You can buy it from most supermarkets or a specialty grocer.

Net carbs: 7 g | Protein: 31 g | Fat: 32 g

100 g (3½ oz) hot-smoked, hot peppered salmon, flaked

100 g (⅔ cup) diced capsicum (bell pepper) – a mix of red and yellow, if possible

55 g (1½ cups) mixed salad greens

2 tablespoons diced red onion

CAJUN DRESSING

2 tablespoons mayonnaise

2 teaspoons lemon juice

½ teaspoon Cajun seasoning

¼ teaspoon minced garlic

1 Toss the salad ingredients together and tip into your lunchbox.

2 Combine the dressing ingredients in a small jar or container with a tight-fitting lid.

3 Pour the dressing over the salad just before serving and toss well.

TUNA & FENNEL SALAD

~~~

This is a salad for the crunch lovers. Using a mandoline will give you perfectly uniform, feather-thin shavings of fennel – just be careful of your fingers!

◇◇◇◇◇◇◇◇◇◇

Net carbs: 6 g | **Protein:** 26 g | **Fat:** 36 g

---

125 g (4½ oz) tinned tuna slices in olive oil, drained

1 celery stalk, thinly sliced

50 g (⅓ cup) shaved fennel, plus a few fronds

handful of shredded radicchio leaves

2 tablespoons toasted flaked almonds

LEMON VINAIGRETTE

1½ tablespoons extra virgin olive oil

1 tablespoon lemon juice

salt and pepper, to taste

1. Toss the salad ingredients together and tip into your lunchbox.

2. Combine the dressing ingredients in a small jar or container with a tight-fitting lid.

3. Pour the dressing over the salad just before serving and toss well.

SMOKED TROUT SALAD

~~~~~~

Smoked trout is a fabulous alternative to other more common tinned or smoked fish options. It's not only a great source of protein, but is also stacked with omega–3 fatty acids, vitamins and nutrients.

◇◇◇◇◇◇◇◇◇◇

Net carbs: 10 g | Protein: 29 g | Fat: 19 g

100 g (3½ oz) smoked trout slices

130 g (4½ oz) short cucumber, halved lengthways and sliced

60 g (2 oz) raw asparagus spears, woody ends trimmed, thinly sliced

50 g (1½ cups) shredded iceberg lettuce

4 cherry tomatoes, halved

2–3 heirloom radishes, thinly sliced

YOGHURT RANCH DRESSING

2 tablespoons Greek-style yoghurt

1 tablespoon mayonnaise

1 teaspoon apple cider vinegar

1 teaspoon chopped dill

1 teaspoon chopped chives

1 teaspoon chopped tarragon

pinch of onion powder

salt and pepper, to taste

1. Toss the salad ingredients together and tip into your lunchbox.

2. Combine the dressing ingredients in a small jar or container with a tight-fitting lid.

3. Pour the dressing over the salad just before serving and toss well.

PRAWN & FLAKED SALMON SALAD

This is a real treat of a salad for seafood lovers. You can swap the hot smoked salmon for left-over cooked salmon, or omit it altogether and double the prawns.

◇◇◇◇◇◇◇◇◇◇

Net carbs: 8 g | Protein: 43 g | Fat: 24 g

½ avocado, diced

100 g (3½ oz) short cucumber, diced

75 g (2¾ oz) cooked peeled prawns (shrimp)

75 g (2¾ oz) hot-smoked salmon, flaked

50 g (1½ cups) chopped cos (romaine) lettuce

2 tablespoons chopped coriander (cilantro) leaves

CREAMY LIME JALAPEÑO DRESSING

2 tablespoons sour cream

1 tablespoon lime juice

pinch of lime zest

1 teaspoon chopped pickled jalapeño

salt and pepper, to taste

1. Toss the salad ingredients together and tip into your lunchbox.

2. Combine the dressing ingredients in a small jar or container with a tight-fitting lid.

3. Pour the dressing over the salad just before serving and toss well.

TUNA POKE

~~~~

A Hawaiian dish made with diced raw fish, rice and vegetables, poke has gained popularity around the world. It can be made keto-friendly by simply swapping steamed white rice for cauliflower rice.

◇◇◇◇◇◇◇◇◇◇

Net carbs: 10 g | **Protein:** 30 g | **Fat:** 37 g

---

150 g (1½ cups) cauliflower rice

100 g (3½ oz) raw sashimi-grade tuna, diced

½ avocado, diced

½ short cucumber, diced

2 radishes, thinly sliced

1 spring onion (scallion), sliced

½ teaspoon toasted sesame seeds

SPICY SRIRACHA MAYO

2½ tablespoons mayonnaise

2 teaspoons rice wine vinegar or lime juice

1 teaspoon sriracha chilli sauce

1 Place the cauliflower rice in your lunchbox and top with the remaining salad ingredients.

2 Combine the dressing ingredients in a small jar or container with a tight-fitting lid.

3 Pour the dressing over the salad just before serving and toss well.

SMOKED SALMON 'BAGEL' SALAD

Classic bagels are a no-no on the keto diet, but you can satisfy your salmon bagel fix at any time with this simple salad. 'Everything bagel' seasoning is available from most supermarkets – or make your own by mixing sesame seeds, poppy seeds, dried garlic and onion flakes with some sea salt.

◇◇◇◇◇◇◇◇◇◇

Net carbs: 9 g | **Protein:** 19 g | **Fat:** 19 g

½ avocado, diced

80 g (2¾ oz) smoked salmon slices

70 g (2 cups) rocket (arugula) or watercress leaves

¼ red onion, thinly sliced

2 teaspoons baby capers

1 teaspoon toasted sesame seeds

lemon wedge, to serve

SOUR CREAM DRESSING

2 tablespoons sour cream

1 tablespoon lemon juice

1 teaspoon 'everything bagel' seasoning mix

1 Toss the salad ingredients together, except the lemon wedge, and tip into your lunchbox. Add the lemon wedge.

2 Whisk the dressing ingredients until smooth, then place in a small jar or container with a tight-fitting lid.

3 Squeeze the lemon wedge over the salad just before serving. Pour the dressing over and toss well to combine.

PRAWN ASPARAGUS SALAD

Asparagus is at its best in spring, and this tasty salad is a simple way to make the most of it. You can blanch the asparagus spears before thinly slicing them, but they are wonderful raw – especially in peak season.

Net carbs: 8 g | Protein: 41 g | Fat: 26 g

100 g (3½ oz) cooked peeled prawns (shrimp)

100 g (3½ oz) raw asparagus spears, woody ends trimmed, thinly sliced lengthways

50 g (1½ cups) watercress leaves

30 g (¼ cup) shaved parmesan

1 tablespoon toasted almond flakes

pinch of lemon zest

CREAMY DIJONNAISE DRESSING

2 tablespoons dijonnaise

1 tablespoon lemon juice

1 tablespoon chopped chives

salt and pepper, to taste

1. Toss the salad ingredients together and tip into your lunchbox.

2. Combine the dressing ingredients in a small jar or container with a tight-fitting lid.

3. Pour the dressing over the salad just before serving.

TUNA & SPINACH SALAD

〜〜〜

This simple salad is packed with protein and healthy fats to keep you full, with plenty of fibre to aid digestion. Dijonnaise is stocked in the condiment aisle of your supermarket and adds a gentle kick to this zesty dressing.

◇◇◇◇◇◇◇◇◇◇

Net carbs: 9 g | **Protein:** 34 g | **Fat:** 49 g

95 g (3¼ oz) tinned tuna in olive oil, drained

2 boiled eggs, halved

2 feta-stuffed baby peppers in olive oil, halved

75 g (1½ cups) baby spinach leaves

2 teaspoons toasted pine nuts

CREAMY LEMON VINAIGRETTE

1 tablespoon extra virgin olive oil

2 teaspoons lemon juice

1 teaspoon dijonnaise

salt and pepper, to taste

1 Toss the salad ingredients together and tip into your lunchbox.

2 Whisk the dressing ingredients until smooth, then place in a small jar or container with a tight-fitting lid.

3 Pour the dressing over the salad just before serving and toss well.

PRAWN CABBAGE SALAD

~~~

Red cabbage is a delicious and economical high-fibre base for salads. The tahini dressing is sweet and salty, with added umami from the miso paste. This salad would be great with chicken or tofu if you're not a big fan of prawns.

◇◇◇◇◇◇◇◇◇◇◇

Net carbs: 16 g | **Protein:** 36 g | **Fat:** 26 g

130 g (¾ cup) chopped cucumber

100 g (3½ oz) cooked peeled prawns (shrimp), sliced

handful of shredded red cabbage

small handful of mint leaves

small handful of coriander (cilantro) leaves

2 tablespoons chopped roasted salted almonds

2 teaspoons toasted sesame seeds

TAHINI GINGER MISO DRESSING

4 teaspoons tahini

1 tablespoon orange juice

1 tablespoon water

1 teaspoon white (shiro) miso paste

½ teaspoon minced ginger

1 Toss the salad ingredients together and tip into your lunchbox.

2 Whisk the dressing ingredients until smooth, then place in a small jar or container with a tight-fitting lid.

3 Pour the dressing over the salad just before serving and toss well.

SASHIMI TUNA SALAD

~~~

When you get your hands on some fresh sashimi-grade tuna from your fishmonger or seafood market, this is the perfect dish to make.

◇◇◇◇◇◇◇◇◇◇

Net carbs: 7 g | Protein: 27 g | Fat: 19 g

100 g (3½ oz) sashimi-grade tuna, thinly sliced

½ short cucumber, halved lengthways and sliced

70 g (½ cup) shirataki noodles, prepared as per packet instructions

3 radishes, thinly sliced

handful of Asian herbs

4 store-bought nori seaweed crisps

GINGER DRESSING

1 tablespoon finely diced shallot

1 tablespoon tamari

1 tablespoon sesame oil

2 teaspoons rice wine vinegar

1 teaspoon minced ginger

1 Toss the salad ingredients together and tip into your lunchbox.

2 Combine the dressing ingredients in a small jar or container with a tight-fitting lid.

3 Pour the dressing over the salad just before serving.

CHIPOTLE PRAWN SALAD

Chipotle sauce adds smoky richness and subtle heat to this Mexican-inspired salad bowl. Queso fresco is a Mexican fresh cheese sold in some delicatessens, but if you can't find it you can just use a mild feta instead.

◇◇◇◇◇◇◇◇◇◇

Net carbs: 8 g | Protein: 34 g | Fat: 16 g

100 g (3½ oz) cooked peeled prawns (shrimp)

1–2 teaspoons chipotle sauce, or to taste

3 radishes, thinly sliced

70 g (2 cups) chopped cos (romaine) lettuce

45 g (1½ oz) queso fresco or feta, crumbled

small handful of coriander (cilantro) leaves

lime wedge, to serve

GUACAMOLE LIME DRESSING

2 tablespoons store-bought guacamole

1 tablespoon lime juice

1 tablespoon sour cream

1. Toss the prawns in a small bowl with the chipotle sauce, coating well. Toss the radish, lettuce, cheese and coriander together and tip into your lunchbox, placing the prawns and lime wedge on top.

2. Whisk the dressing ingredients until smooth, then place in a small jar or container with a tight-fitting lid.

3. Squeeze the lime wedge over the salad just before serving. Dollop the dressing over and toss well to combine.

CLASSICS + NEW CLASSICS

CLASSIC CAPRESE SALAD

It's hard to think of a simpler salad, but the classic caprese is far greater than the sum of its parts. Use the freshest, ripest tomatoes you can get your hands on to really make this salad sing.

Net carbs: 7 g | Protein: 12 g | Fat: 43 g

2 roma (plum) tomatoes, sliced

60 g (2 oz) fresh mozzarella, sliced or torn

small handful of basil leaves

1 tablespoon toasted pine nuts

PESTO DRESSING

2 tablespoons store-bought pesto

2 teaspoons extra virgin olive oil

1–2 teaspoons lemon juice, to taste

1. Toss the salad ingredients together and tip into your lunchbox.

2. Combine the dressing ingredients in a small jar or container with a tight-fitting lid.

3. Spoon the dressing over the salad just before serving and toss well.

CREAMY EGG SALAD WITH LETTUCE CUPS

Eggs are one of the most nutritious protein sources and are loaded with almost every vitamin and mineral needed by the human body. They're also an excellent source of healthy fats, making them a perfect choice for keto-friendly lunches.

✕✕✕✕✕✕✕✕✕✕

Net carbs: 5 g | **Protein:** 15 g | **Fat:** 32 g

2 hard-boiled eggs, chopped

70 g (½ cup) finely chopped celery

1 spring onion (scallion), thinly sliced

1 tablespoon chopped parsley

4–5 baby cos (romaine) lettuce leaves

CREAMY MUSTARD DRESSING

2 tablespoons mayonnaise

1 teaspoon dijon mustard

1 teaspoon apple cider vinegar

salt and pepper, to taste

1. In a bowl, combine the egg, celery, spring onion and parsley.

2. Mix together the dressing ingredients and gently toss through the salad.

3. Pop the salad into your lunchbox and store the lettuce leaves separately.

4. Spoon the egg salad into your lettuce leaves just before serving.

CHICKEN CAESAR SALAD

Here you'll find all the flavours of the classic caesar you know and love, but with the ease of a 5-minute salad. Crunchy pork crackles (also called chicharrones or pork rinds) have replaced bacon here for a quick and easy crunchy element.

◇◇◇◇◇◇◇◇◇◇

Net carbs: 4 g | **Protein:** 65 g | **Fat:** 44 g

120 g (4½ oz) shredded cooked chicken

70 g (2 cups) chopped cos (romaine) lettuce

30 g (¼ cup) shaved parmesan

20 g (¾ oz) crunchy pork rinds, crumbled

2–3 white anchovy fillets in oil, drained and sliced

CREAMY CAESAR DRESSING

2 tablespoons mayonnaise

1 tablespoon finely grated parmesan

2 teaspoons lemon juice

½ teaspoon worcestershire sauce

¼ teaspoon minced garlic

salt and pepper, to taste

1 Toss the salad ingredients together and tip into your lunchbox.

2 Combine the dressing ingredients in a small jar or container with a tight-fitting lid.

3 Pour the dressing over the salad just before serving and toss well.

COBB SALAD

Cobb salad is a classic American dish that dates back to 1930s Hollywood. Keeping it lunchbox-friendly means you probably won't have the toppings arranged in the signature rows, but this version has all the right flavours.

◇◇◇◇◇◇◇◇◇◇

Net carbs: 7 g | Protein: 54 g | Fat: 45 g

1 tomato, diced

100 g (3½ oz) cooked chicken, diced

¼ avocado, diced

50 g (1½ cups) chopped cos (romaine) lettuce

30 g (1 oz) blue cheese, crumbled

25 g (1 oz) cooked bacon, chopped

1 hard-boiled egg, quartered

ONION & MUSTARD VINAIGRETTE

1 tablespoon extra virgin olive oil

1 tablespoon chopped red onion

2 teaspoons red wine vinegar

1 teaspoon dijon mustard

salt and pepper, to taste

1 Toss the salad ingredients together and tip into your lunchbox.

2 Combine the dressing ingredients in a small jar or container with a tight-fitting lid.

3 Pour the dressing over the salad just before serving and toss well.

SARDINE NIÇOISE

~~~

This play on a keto-friendly niçoise salad uses sardines
instead of tinned tuna. Sardines are an excellent lunchtime
protein option, being full of omega–3 fatty acids, which
have been linked to improved brain and heart health.

◇◇◇◇◇◇◇◇◇◇

Net carbs: 8 g | Protein: 26 g | Fat: 28 g

---

110 g (4 oz) tinned sardines in oil,
drained

3 white anchovy fillets in olive oil

½ short cucumber, cut into chunks

6 cherry tomatoes, halved

8 pitted marinated olives

4 caper berries, sliced

20 g (½ cup) rocket (arugula)
leaves

lemon wedge, to serve

SIMPLE LEMON DRESSING

1 tablespoon extra virgin olive oil

2 teaspoons lemon juice

salt and pepper, to taste

1 Toss the salad ingredients together,
except the lemon wedge, and tip into
your lunchbox. Add the lemon wedge.

2 Combine the dressing ingredients
in a small jar or container with a
tight-fitting lid.

3 Squeeze the lemon wedge over
the salad just before serving.
Pour the dressing over and toss
well to combine.

ANTIPASTO SALAD

〰️

This salad is super simple to put together and relies on some of the yummiest keto-friendly items from your local deli. You can dial up the heat by using a spicy salami, if you wish.

◇◇◇◇◇◇◇◇◇◇

Net carbs: 7 g | Protein: 24 g | Fat: 69 g

70 g (2½ oz) sliced pork salami

50 g (1½ cups) rocket (arugula) leaves

3 bocconcini, halved

4 cherry tomatoes, halved

8 marinated pitted olives

3 pepperoncini (marinated hot yellow peppers), sliced, stems discarded

ITALIAN VINAIGRETTE

2 tablespoons extra virgin olive oil

1 tablespoon red wine vinegar

1 tablespoon finely diced red onion

½ teaspoon dried Italian herbs

salt and pepper, to taste

1 Toss the salad ingredients together and tip into your lunchbox.

2 Combine the dressing ingredients in a small jar or container with a tight-fitting lid.

3 Pour the dressing over the salad just before serving and toss well.

HAM & CHEESE SALAD

~

When you're craving a ham and cheese sandwich for lunch, try this instead! Eggs are a satisfying low-carb addition to your lunchtime salads, with two large hard-boiled eggs containing around 13 g protein, 11 g fat and just over 1 g of carbs.

◇◇◇◇◇◇◇◇◇◇

Net carbs: 7 g | Protein: 40 g | Fat: 38 g

2 hard-boiled eggs, quartered

80 g (2¾ oz) shaved ham, sliced

50 g (1¾ oz) smoked mozzarella, grated

50 g (1½ cups) chopped cos (romaine) lettuce

1 spring onion (scallion), sliced

CREAMY ITALIAN DRESSING

2 teaspoons sour cream

2 teaspoons extra virgin olive oil

1 teaspoon balsamic vinegar

½ teaspoon dried Italian herbs

¼ teaspoon minced garlic

salt and pepper, to taste

1. Toss the salad ingredients together and tip into your lunchbox.

2. Combine the dressing ingredients in a small jar or container with a tight-fitting lid.

3. Pour the dressing over the salad just before serving and toss well.

CRISPY PROSCIUTTO & SHAVED BRUSSELS SPROUT SALAD

Brussels sprouts have been much maligned, but when you thinly shave them, you could almost mistake them for cabbage. Crispy prosciutto takes this salad to the next level. Simply cook the prosciutto in a non-stick frying pan for 2 minutes until crispy, or microwave between two sheets of paper towel for 30 seconds.

Net carbs: 9 g | Protein: 18 g | Fat: 34 g

3 slices prosciutto, fried until crisp and crumbled, see note above

100 g (2 cups) shaved brussels sprouts

5 cherry tomatoes, halved

1 hard-boiled egg, quartered

1 tablespoon diced red onion

1 tablespoon toasted pine nuts

TANGY DIJON DRESSING

1½ tablespoons extra virgin olive oil

1 tablespoons apple cider vinegar

¼ teaspoon dijon mustard

salt and pepper, to taste

1. Toss the salad ingredients together and tip into your lunchbox.

2. Combine the dressing ingredients in a small jar or container with a tight-fitting lid.

3. Pour the dressing over the salad just before serving and toss well.

TURKEY SALAD

〰️

Packed with protein from the turkey and Swiss cheese, and healthy fats from the avocado, this salad will help ensure you avoid the dreaded mid-afternoon slump.

◇◇◇◇◇◇◇◇◇◇

Net carbs: 7 g | Protein: 29 g | Fat: 38 g

---

80 g (2¾ oz) shaved turkey
50 g (1¾ oz) Swiss cheese, shredded
¼ avocado, diced
5 cherry tomatoes, halved
30 g (¾ cup) rocket (arugula) leaves
handful of alfalfa sprouts

DIJON & CHAMPAGNE VINEGAR DRESSING

1 tablespoon extra virgin olive oil
2 teaspoons finely diced shallot or red onion
2 teaspoons champagne vinegar
1 teaspoon dijon mustard
salt and pepper, to taste

1. Toss the salad ingredients together and tip into your lunchbox.

2. Combine the dressing ingredients in a small jar or container with a tight-fitting lid.

3. Pour the dressing over the salad just before serving and toss well.

TOFU TACO SALAD

~

Plain tofu can be a little flavourless on its own, but mixing it with smoky chipotle sauce in the morning gives the tofu several hours to take on plenty of flavour, with barely any effort on your part.

◇◇◇◇◇◇◇◇◇◇◇

Net carbs: 12 g | Protein: 16 g | Fat: 24 g

100 g (3½ oz) firm tofu, drained and diced

1 tablespoon chipotle sauce

½ avocado, diced

50 g (1½ cups) shredded iceberg lettuce

5 cherry tomatoes, halved

2 radishes, sliced

1 tablespoon pumpkin seeds

LIME & SOUR CREAM DRESSING

2 tablespoons sour cream

1 tablespoon lime juice

2 teaspoons chopped coriander (cilantro) leaves

pinch of onion powder

salt and pepper, to taste

1. Toss the tofu in a bowl with the chipotle sauce, coating well. Combine with the remaining salad ingredients and tip into your lunchbox.

2. Combine the dressing ingredients in a small jar or container with a tight-fitting lid.

3. Pour the dressing over the salad just before serving and toss well.

BERRY SALAD LUNCHBOX

〜〜〜

Here's a great bring-to-work breakfast option for those of us who find it difficult to eat something balanced in the mornings before the workday begins. Packing the coconut flakes and almonds separately keeps them crunchy for serving.

◇◇◇◇◇◇◇◇◇◇

Net carbs: 16 g | **Protein:** 19 g | **Fat:** 19 g

125 g (4½ oz) full-fat cottage cheese

generous pinch of cinnamon

150 g (5½ oz) mixed fresh berries, such as strawberries, blackberries and raspberries

1 tablespoon orange juice

¼ teaspoon vanilla bean paste or extract

2 tablespoons toasted coconut flakes

1½ tablespoons slivered almonds

small handful of mint leaves

1. Place the cottage cheese in a small jar or container and sprinkle with the cinnamon. Seal and place in your lunchbox.

2. Toss the berries with the orange juice and vanilla and tip them into your lunchbox.

3. Pack the remaining ingredients separately and scatter over the salad just before serving.

INDEX

Salads by net carb quantity

Published in 2025 by Smith Street Books
Naarm (Melbourne) | Australia
smithstreetbooks.com

ISBN: 978-1-9230-4979-6 (Hardcase)
ISBN: 978-1-9232-3909-8 (Flexicase)

Smith Street Books respectfully acknowledges the Wurundjeri People of the Kulin Nation, who are the Traditional Owners of the land on which we work, and we pay our respects to their Elders past and present.

Disclaimer: The information in this book does not negate the personal responsibility of the reader for their own health and safety. The opinion of a medical professional should be sought for tailored advice before commencing a change in diet. The publishers and their employees are not liable for any injury or damage incurred from reading or following the information in this book.

Nutrition information been calculated based off of the USDA FoodData Central Database and the Nutrition Coordinating Center Food & Nutrition Database.

Publisher: Paul McNally
Editor: Katri Hilden
Project editor: Elena Callcott
Series design: Kate Barraclough
Additional design: George Saad
Layout: Megan Ellis
Photographer: Daniel Herrmann-Zoll
Food stylist: Deborah Kaloper
Proofreader: Pamela Dunne
Indexer: Helena Holmgren

Printed & bound in China by C&C Offset Printing Co., Ltd.

Book 366
10 9 8 7 6 5 4 3 2 1